MAX VERSTAPPEN

HOW MAX VERSTAPPEN BECAME THE FASTEST

DRIVER IN FORMULA ONE

By

JACKSON CARTER

Copyright © 2021

TABLE OF CONTENTS

Legal Notes

Max Verstappen is meant for entertainment and educational use only. All attempts have been made to present factual information in an unbiased context.

DRIVING IN THE DNA

When your parents are both professionals in their sport like Max Verstappen's, you'd think that your DNA would be enough to become a pro too. Or maybe not. Maybe the pressure to follow in their hefty footsteps would simply be too much for you. Or maybe the "tough love" you received at home would make you turn completely in another direction.

This is the short story of the aforementioned Max, a Dutch-Belgian race car driver, who's on the verge of winning a Formula 1 world championship and what he's chosen to do with his DNA and his life.

Still only 23 years of age, Verstappen is simultaneously one of F1's current shooting stars and a driver who could continue his dominance all the way into the distant 2030s. Seemingly from nowhere, he burst onto the racing scene in 2015 as a precocious prodigy.

"He has unbelievable speed," Helmut Marko, Red Bull's motorsport advisor, affirmed at the time. "He is very mature for his age and he's a hard worker. He has all the ingredients you need to be an absolute champion."

If somebody totally in the know says that an F1 driver has "unbelievable speed," it means that his race car hits velocities that are really fast and extremely dangerous. Given the fact that F1 cars can reach top speeds of 240 miles per hour (390 kph)—more than three times faster than the maximum speed for cars on any American freeway—and an average pace of 164 mph (264 kph) on the world's speedway circuit, they demand a very special breed of skilled pilots. It's not simply a walk in the park on a lazy Sunday.

Verstappen made his F1 debut after only one year of official car racing, making the leap up from karts to European Formula 3. With open, four-wheeled vehicles, karting might seem like it's for kids. Yet, this sort of racing is typically seen as the launching pad to the higher levels of motorsports.

Former F1 champs like Sebastian Vettel, Nico Rosberg, Ayrton Senna, Lewis Hamilton, Michael Schumacher, Kimi Raikkonen, and Fernando Alonso all kick-started their careers in karting.

Max's journey to the top may seem abrupt, but it hasn't been quite like that. At the tender age of four, he began to roll down this championship pathway.

MAX'S KID DAYS

The racing bug bit at an early age. It all started with the familiar story of a kid fascinated with vehicles but held back by slightly concerned and reticent parents. Verstappen got into driving quad bikes when he was still just two.

At the age of four, he saw a smaller friend karting and immediately asked his father if he could play with a kart too. Apparently, Max understood the desire to "keep up with the Joneses" (or the Janssens, as the case may be in Belgium) quite early on.

Dutch dad, Jos, initially resisted, but the boy's constant pleading—and a few tears shed for good measure—helped get his mom on his side. Ultimately, the Verstappen adults gave in, placing Max in the driver's seat of a kart for the first time at four and a half years old. "It was at Genk, it was on the rental circuit, and it was with a very small go-kart," Jos recalled in a 2020 interview with Red Bull.

"We still have it. It's hanging in the shop where we sell merchandise. But I remember after a few laps, he did the whole track flat out. And because of the vibration of the kart, the carburetor was falling off all the time. We did it for one day, and then immediately bought him a bigger go-kart," Max's father chuckled.

The kid inside each of us surely remembers the time when we first thrilled at the sensation of speed, whether it was aboard a go-kart, a mini-bike, or maybe even a whizzing tricycle—that incomparable feeling of freedom and excitement, careening just on the edge of control. However, not everyone has the chance, or the guts, to go quite as fast as Max.

As well as having a famously fleet father, Max's Belgian mother, Sophie Kumpen, was also an accomplished kart driver. Verstappen the father took part in a total of 107 Grand Prix races in his career. He was able to climb the podium twice and managed to score 17 championship points (calculated as 117 in the modern system) all told, making him the second-best Dutch driver in F1 history to date, eclipsed only by the boy we're introducing to you now: Max.

Seen as a fearsome opponent by his contemporaries, Jos was both fast and combative, often winding up in close encounters with gravel traps. To shed some light on this particular patch you see on the sides of race tracks: when cars enter the gravel pit at high speed, the uneven surface sometimes causes them to roll over, resulting in a large amount of damage and debris.

Drivers don't like gravel pits because they can get unforgivingly stuck in 'the gravel trap'. Then, if the race marshals choose not to quickly help out, or the engine shuts off, your race is over. It's also widely known that Jos's raw talent and indisputable desire were reined in by 'inferior machinery' while driving with sponsors such as Simtek, Footwork, Tyrrell, Stewart, Arrows, and Minardi.

In a seriously competitive car with the Benetton team, driving alongside the incomparable Michael Schumacher in 1994, the world caught glances of Max's father's real talent that podium finishes in Hungary and Belgium attested to.

However, Jos is perhaps best remembered as the destitute protagonist in a dramatic pit lane inferno during the German Grand Prix at Hockenheim in 1994. This brings up the question: what about the inherent risks of this derring-do sport?

After watching replays of the dramatic footage of his father's Benetton car being engulfed by flames with Jos still wedged inside the simmering cockpit, inhaling suffocating fumes before a narrow escape, does Max ever question the safety and sanity of his chosen profession nowadays?

"I've seen the fire. Those things can happen—at least when we had re-fueling. It's part of racing," he retorted in a matter-of-fact fashion. "There are always accidents in racing. This is what we do as race drivers. These are the risks."

Verstappen senior even traveled to the Japanese Grand Prix in Suzuka to race for the Tyrrell team only ten days after his son was born in late 1997. A bit later, Verstappen junior was spied at karting circuits basically before he could walk. "One of my first racing memories was in Malaysia. My dad was racing and I was there, running around in the paddock as well. I think I was like three years old or something," Max said, smiling.

AN EARLY START TO RACING

Born in September 1997 in Hasselt, Belgium, it didn't take Max Emilian very long to settle into the habit of winning races. He won his first race at the age of seven. The lad quickly became a champion in both Belgium and the Netherlands at age nine, and would go on to add more domestic titles over the next several years.

By age 13, he'd already romped to a trio of WSK titles in his first year competing in Europe and finished second in the CIK-FIA World Cup behind his future Red Bull teammate, Alexander Albon, who holds dual Thai and British citizenship. But Max didn't give up easily, soon beating Albon in a Euro Series race.

By his sweet sixteenth year, which was his last year karting while he eased into the senior categories at the same time, he was named the European and World champion in car racing's two most competitive and professional classes, including the always fast and furious F1.

"Max has an extraordinary mastery of the vehicle," Verstappen's CRG team boss, Giancarlo Tinini, told TKART magazine in 2010. "Few racers are able to make the difference in the first two laps of a race. He is one of them."

From Max's preliminary kart adventures leading up to his eventual world championship success, Jos the elder threw everything into his son's fledgling career. He sweated over fine-tuning his chassis and engines during the day in his workshop, while Max was off having a go at school. Then they would head out together to test the sensitive mechanical stuff two or three times a week.

They drove in excess of 62,000 miles (some 100,000 kilometers) a year on the racing circuit, keeping each other company in a well-worn van. They crisscrossed Belgium and the Netherlands, as well as way beyond. "We knew exactly which engine was the best and knew what carburetors were richer, so everything was sorted," Jos recollected.

"I knew exactly which engine we had to use and things like that. And of course, Max had to set up the carburetors for that. That's a feeling a driver needs to have. And I think he was very good at that. He was very precise on what he liked to have in his kart," his father concluded.

This kind of practical education seemed better received by Max than his actual schooling. "Especially when you start driving internationally, it becomes quite difficult to keep up to speed with school," Max quipped—not exactly what his testy teachers wanted to hear. "From when I was like 11, 12 years old, it became quite tricky."

With any kind of racing, some onlookers will always ask: Who or what's really winning the race? Is it the driver only, or the car, or perhaps the pit crew or team? "I'm not the person who likes to work on the engine. My dad really enjoys doing that. I have always loved driving more. But I think it's really important that you understand what's going on. I was always involved, looking at what my dad was doing, and understanding what he was doing. But I never had that feeling of doing it myself," Max emphasized, setting the record straight.

The younger Verstappen got used to that working rhythm during his karting 'apprenticeship'. Soon, the Verstappen family teamed up with the Pex Racing Team, a customer of CRG (the well-known chassis maker), and operated out of their trackside tent. But the father-and-son squad stayed principally in charge of their own machinery. Jos continued to prepare the engines himself, harnessing his own 'dyno,' a device used to measure the force, torque, and horsepower of a vehicle's engine.

"I don't think many people had the guidance from a very young age like I had," reflected Max. "They catch up, they learn a lot. But from a very young age, I just learned a lot straight away."

That constant learning process turned out to be much more than Jos insisting that his son should have a total understanding of the mechanical side. Driving was always the number one priority. Jos himself had never quite climbed to the F1 heights he'd hoped for and hence was determined to make sure that Max became a much better driver than him.

Besides, what do you think happens when you're born to parents of different nationalities and you grow up on the border between two European nations that are culturally and linguistically similar?

Even though Max's mom is Belgian and he himself was born in Belgium and resided as a youngster in Berr in that country, he decided to enter competitions using a Dutch racing license. That's because he claims he "feels more Dutch".

Indeed, he spent more time with his father than with his mother due to his non-stop karting activities, and always hung around with lots of Dutch people while growing up in Maaseik, a Belgian town located on the border with Holland.

"I actually only lived in Belgium to sleep. But during the day, I went to the Netherlands and had my friends there too. I was raised as a Dutch person and that's how I feel,"

Max admitted in 2015. He officially went with the Dutch nationality when he turned the age of majority.

He also competed in F1 for more than half a season before he was given a driver's license for the real road on his eighteenth birthday. Max had made Monaco, France his home since October of 2015, though he claimed it isn't merely for "tax management" purposes, as some would have it. Monaco is home to one of F1's most challenging circuits, filled with plenty of tight turns. The city also boasts casinos, malls, museums, and palaces, as well as marvelous Mediterranean beaches reclaimed from the sea.

Whether Max's DNA leans more to the Belgian or Dutch side of the border remains a talking point. But Max's mom definitely had her hand in the mix. Sophie Kumpen herself first got into kart racing at the age of

10 after watching her uncle, Paul Kumpen, in Rallycross. By the time she was 16, Kumpen was viewed as an up-and-coming talent, competing in the Formula A World Championship, ultimately crossing the finish line in ninth.

The next year, in 1992, Kumpen cruised in the Karting World Championship, wrapping up the season in 26th place, just ahead of F1 driver, Giancarlo Fisichella. She continued to figure in the Karting World Championship, managing a reasonable 17th place finish in 1994.

But the highlight of Kumpen's racing career was her astonishing haul of the Andrea Margutti Trophy in 1995 when she conspired to beat the likes of Jarno Trulli and the late Allan Simonsen. During the 1995 campaign, Kumpen also became teammates with future F1 World Champion,

Jenson Button, and the pair often found themselves racing against each other.

Speaking on the official F1 podcast *Beyond The Grid*, Button boasted lavishly of Kumpen's motoring skills: "Sophie, Max's mum, was a fantastic driver. When I was racing in karts in 1995, she was my teammate, so I saw her drive. I knew how good she was.

"It was her and the late Lotta Hellberg—those two were just awesome—so fast," Button waxed. He wasn't the only member of racing royalty to heap praises on Kumpen. Max's team principal at Red Bull, Christian Horner, remembered: "I raced against his mum. In 1989, I raced against her in the Junior Kart World Championship. In that race, there were some super-talented drivers, such as Jan Magnussen, Jarno Trulli, Giancarlo

Fisichella, and Franchitti. She was top 10 in the world, for sure."

Kumpen herself had lofty dreams of making it as an F1 driver, but developments in her personal life made her decide otherwise. In 1996, Kumpen married Dutch race driver, Jos Verstappen. They went on to have two children—Max in 1997 and his sister, Victoria, in 1999 (by the way, Max's younger sister currently has a considerable following on social media and her own fashion line). Raising her children while simultaneously supporting her husband's F1 efforts, Kumpen cut her own racing career short at the age of 21.

Revealing her momentous decision to *F1 Wags*, Kumpen recalled: "I wanted to go to F1. I tested some race cars, then I married Max's dad, and I had to make a choice. He was driving F1 and, at that time, we were away so much. So, I gave up my dream. But now I see my son realizing what I wanted to do and I enjoy it as much."

Nowadays, with the "W-Series" being contested as Formula 1 support races for the first time, and female motorsport surging in popularity every year, it's worth celebrating the accomplishments of female racers like Kumpen, Hellberg, and Susanna Raganelli. All of them challenged the status quo and raced extremely fast, long before anyone was actively championing women.

WHAT IS 'TOUGH LOVE' REALLY?

Max and his father, Jos, obviously enjoy a relatively good relationship with one another. On the other hand, the young Dutchman has revealed that both his parents were hard-nosed, resilient taskmasters. That was the case in particular with his father, a former F1 driver, and we're not just talking about Max cleaning up his bedroom once a week.

Just after the Russian Grand Prix 2019 in Sochi, Max reminisced about an intriguing event from his bygone karting days. In 2012, when he was just 15 years old, he was entered to race in an event in Sarno, close to Naples, Italy.

"I should have won that race easily," he explained to *The Daily Telegraph*. "On the first lap, someone overtook me and I wanted to regain my position on the next lap. I tried to pass on a very fast turn. He didn't see me and we collided. My dad worked very hard that weekend and I threw it all away. He was very angry and didn't talk to me. On the way home, about five miles away, he said something to me and we ended up arguing."

Suddenly, Jos pulled into a gas station and proceeded to kick his son out of the van, according to what Max remembered. His dad insisted that he find his way home alone, and left the 15-year-old standing at the station as the van roared off. Rather than walking back to his house, Max called his mother to pick him up. Matters remained tense on the home front, and he and Jos weren't on speaking terms for at least a week.

"I never had any surprises in F1 because no one was as hard on me as my dad," the rising star stressed to all those listening. Some familiar-sounding anecdotes emerge from this period in the Verstappens' lives: Jos sending Max out after modifying certain things on the kart without telling him, in an effort to improve his feedback, or continuing to test vehicles even when rain started to fall and most of the others packed up and went home.

There were also less conventional methods that the father recalls: "Even in races, I told him because he was winning so easily. For example, I told him that he couldn't overtake in a certain corner or certain part on the track. So, he had to find different spots to do that. It was just to make it more difficult for him, to find other ways to overtake or not."

This type of "feeling" as a driver was vital in Jos's mind: "Especially when you are young." Data had been a rare commodity during his own junior career, but at the same time, he didn't want Max to become too reliant on it as he witnessed fellow racers doing.

He strived to help his son know what to do in as many diverse situations as possible, to understand where the best grip was in wet conditions, what he could see with his eyes in comparison to how things felt through his hands gripping the wheel, and in what ways the kart would react on different angles of approach.

Thus, Max was taught to learn by doing and to figure out limits on his own, but also to realize where the kart could go faster as well. In addition, he was told to never lie: If he didn't really feel some difference, then he should say that. The youngster went along with the process.

"It's funny...even in junior categories, there was quite a big difference in how the teams are operating in terms of the amount of time you spend on the track," Verstappen admitted alongside his father in an interview hosted by ex-racer, David Coulthard, in late 2020.

"Some people would spend more time looking at data. I think we were a bit more of the 'just drive' (type) because you learn while driving. A lot of teams at that time, they're looking at data for 45 minutes," Jos added. "I said to them, 'I don't want that. Five minutes is fine, but give him time on track'. That's what they need; they need to feel the car and make changes to it. But they were more into data."

Max replied: "You can look at a brake graph for 45 minutes, but I'm not changing it. Am I, if I'm looking at it? I have to go to the track and understand and try different things."

Jos then reflected on the lessons he tried to teach his son in a straightforward way: "As a father, you always want to help your son as best as possible. I tried to push him in the right direction."

Sometimes that didn't manifest itself too nicely. He strongly believes that there are many young aspiring athletes and drivers out there who've experienced similar situations. As we hinted earlier, 'karting dads' can be a demanding and particular breed. With the increased investments of time, effort, and money come heightened expectations.

That scenario constantly tested Max in various ways. "I remember he was probably eight or nine or something," Jos recalled. "On Wednesdays, school was finished at 12. We went to the go-kart track and in the wintertime, it was freezing.

"So, I let the van run so he could warm up, and then we did 10 laps. He was cold. I said 'OK, go warm up', and then three minutes later [Max wasn't back] 'F--- (Fudge), where is he now? Come on!' [Then Max would say] 'I'm still cold'. 'I don't care...drive.' And he couldn't move his fingers, and I didn't care. I wanted to test things because I was building engines and changing chassis, and I wanted to have a result because I wanted to move forward," Jos re-enacted the scene.

"I could barely hold the steering wheel," Max interrupted. Jos quickly clarified: "And then, when the fingers warm up again, that's very painful. I said, 'Ah, shut up'." Max chuckled: "Trying to make me tough, I think." Max may have actually been laughing during that later interview. But what about when he really suffered at the hands of his dowdy dad?

It could be a steering wheel for some kids, or maybe a hard hockey stick, or even a cold steel baseball bat in the rain. Can we simply accept it if a father (or mother) shows such tough love in a constant drive to push their kids to greater heights— maybe to achieve something they never could?

'Tough love' is how former Red Bull driver, David Coulthard, hosting the interview, including this particular exchange, termed it. Of course, there are other stories from the same vein. Max tells a peculiar one, from his penultimate year in karts, where after one practice session in which he was "driving like a potato, I swear", he got a solid thump over the crash helmet from his indignant dad in front of all the others.

Imitating his father, Max claimed the message was: "If you don't drive normal, we go home. I'll pack up everything!" In his own defense, Jos pointed out that Max went on to qualify for the pole position, and then to win all his qualifying races as well as the main events. "A nice wake-up call. I needed it," Max quipped.

"But I knew his driving style," continued Jos. "And I can see if he was making bad choices or driving bad—I could see it immediately. It woke him up. He needed that sometimes."

That's been explained away as a slight difference in regular and racing personalities. In 2014, Jos described his own son as "a very good character. He has a gentle character. When he puts his helmet on, it changes. He's more aggressive because he wants to win."

Indeed, the F1 circuit witnessed a more mature Max in 2020 as he was able to handle the frustration of not remaining in the mix for the world championship with a sense of humor and a relaxed demeanor. He even joked in an interview with *The*

Race that it was a lot harder on his dad than him.

For as long as Max can remember, his way of handling expectations and getting the most out of himself was to simply shrug off disappointments and not get too worked up about things, thereby preventing pressure from building up in the first place.

That apparently jarred with Jos. Particularly in his younger days, Max admitted that "My dad sometimes thought I was too relaxed, too easy-going". Jos readily agreed. He recalled that it was "all very easy for him", and he believed that it sometimes meant that Max honestly didn't care enough.

The clearest instance of this was the aforementioned occasion when Jos 'left' Max on his own at the gas station. It happened just after the 2012 CIK-FIA KZ2 World Cup. Max remembers it as "one of the easiest weekends of my career".

On that occasion, he overcame a burned clutch in a qualifying heat and a tenth-place start in the pre-final to win and earned the pole position for the main race. But it all came to nothing when he crashed in the second lap into a racing rival who he was impatiently trying to repass much too quickly and carelessly.

"It was a bit stupid and unnecessary," Max admitted. "So I crashed. No world championship. My dad invested so much time already the years before, preparing the engines, making sure that once I stepped up to that category, that everything would be ready to go. So I was, of course, upset, but my dad was really upset and disappointed in me.

"He broke down the tent—everything. He threw it in the van. I had to pick up the kart with a friend of mine on the track after the race because my dad said I had to do it myself. We sat in the van on our way back home. I wanted to talk to my dad about what happened, my opinion about the incident, but my dad didn't want to talk to me. I kept trying, and at one point, he stopped at a fuel station and he's like, 'Get out! I don't want to talk to you anymore'," recollected the youth.

Here's the complete context: Max's mother happened to be in a separate car a few minutes behind, and Jos swears he never intended to abandon the teen outright. At that point, Max even defended his father, adding, "You came back anyway, so it's all right."

"We drove about 1,800 kilometers back home. I didn't say a word to him," Jos explained. "And the whole week after I didn't speak to him. And then we were sitting together, so I explained to him how I felt. The whole week he didn't feel comfortable with the whole situation. But I wanted him to understand that he had to think.

"The next season we won everything. We won two European Championships, the World Championship; we won every race. He was so focused...the way he was racing, you could see he was thinking, and I think because of what happened at that race, it made him a better driver," the dad asserted.

These are slightly uncomfortable stories for all involved, especially considering the saying that the ends necessarily justify the means. It surely represents a pushy parenting style, at least in terms of competition.

But the younger Verstappen reflects on those memories almost universally with a grin on his smooth face. He believes he's undeniably a better driver because of them.

After all, that was the compelling force behind Jos's most curious and questionable methods: to influence Max as much as possible and make him better than his father ever was.

"He uses his head more and his driving style is more fluent," Jos appraised. "I can be aggressive," Max warned. "I just like to race hard. I think my dad also did that. I think I just have a bit more finesse in my driving style. But that's also what we worked on from when I was very little. My dad wanted me to become better than him."

Does Max see his father as a direct role model? "It's great to have an example. He's still helping me a lot as well. If I have any questions...if I need advice, I can always go to him," Max affirms. "Of course, he's very proud of me, as I think any father would be."

At the risk of getting too far ahead of our story, Max has quickly become an instinctively fast driver, showing great adaptability, aggression, and with each passing season, more maturity and better judgment—a much-needed commodity when you drive sleek-screaming cars at speeds in excess of 223 mph (360 kph) on the straights. By the way, these vehicles can move from a standstill to 60 mph (96.5 kph) in 2.6 seconds, in case you're ever in a hurry to get to the local grocery store.

Valtteri Bottas, from Nastola, Finland, currently holds the record for the greatest speed ever in an F1 race, hitting 231.4 mph (372.5 kph) during the Mexican Grand Prix in 2016. This is surely fast, but F1 cars aren't quite the fastest single-seaters—that award goes to IndyCar.

While an F1 vehicle isn't quite as quick in a straight line, the car that Max drives focuses on downforce and cornering speeds, meaning that F1 cars are, in general, faster than an IndyCar over an entire lap. Without getting into all the aerodynamics involved, with the front and rear wings and the deep tunnels in the floor designed to suck the car close to the track, these autos (space ships?) aren't exactly a cinch to drive.

This phenom named Verstappen is clear proof that a driver's qualities don't come down to just the classic debate of nature versus nurture, but rather both. Even if 'nurture' is too gentle of a word to describe his strict racing education at times, it seems that the same end result could well have been achieved with more humane methods along the way.

The outcome is that Max is currently seen by many pundits in the F1 world as the British champion Lewis Hamilton's heir apparent. That's why both father and son fully approve of the process that's turned Max into the awe-inspiring driver he currently is—as harsh and intense as it was for him (and his dad) at times.

Just in case you were wondering, in a line of legendary F1 champions, Lewis Carl Hamilton was born in Stevenage, England in January 1985. Undoubtedly, Hamilton is one of the most highly acclaimed F1 Grand Prix drivers of all time. He claims the F1 record for career race victories with 91 and is tied with German Michael Schumacher for the drivers with the most championships (seven). In 2008, Lewis became the first Black driver to win the F1 world drivers' championship.

On a sadder note, news about former F1 champion Michael Schumacher's condition remains sketchy after he suffered a horrendous skiing accident in 2013. Following two brain surgeries and an induced coma that lasted six months, he apparently remained in a vegetative state, surrounded by his wife, family, and nurses. To this day, Schumacher still holds the F1 record for the highest number of fastest laps and most races won in a single season (finishing first in 13 of 18 races in his banner year of 2004).

LET'S RACE WITH THE BIG BOYS, PLEASE

When Max was only sweet 16 (years of age that is), he was invited to participate in the Red Bull-sponsored racing program. With nothing left for him to conquer on the karting circuit the previous year, he stepped up to contest in the FIA European Formula 3 Championship.

Built by Mygale, Formula 3 cars typically top out at speeds of about 167 mph (270 kph), making them the 'slowest' fuel-based Formula racing vehicles. They're all designed in a similar way, guaranteeing that driver talent is a much bigger factor than the components or parts of the vehicle in question.

This ensures that F3 races appear much closer than in F1, where a particular vehicle's specs can completely dominate the track and results. Also, since the former vehicles are slower and don't have a "Drag Reduction System", much of the exciting action occurs around the bends of the track.

Against more experienced opposition, Max won a total of ten races on his way to third in the 2014 F3 championship. However, he'd planned his next step long before his first and only season finished. Sixteen-year-old Max joined the Red Bull Junior Team in August and was officially announced as a 2015 race driver for the Italian team referred to as Scuderia Toro Rosso.

After finishing 2014 with three FP1 appearances and a short winter testing program, Max made his Grand Prix debut at the 2015 Australian Grand Prix at the age of 17 years and 166 days—the youngest driver in the history of the sport. Two weeks later, he grabbed another record, becoming the youngest point-scorer in F1 history following a seventh-place finish in Malaysia.

How did Verstappen deal with such immense responsibility at the age of only 17, when most other kids are thinking of how to make it through high school in one piece? "Everything has gone really fast in my life. At the end of the day, I never really think about my age. For me, it doesn't really matter," he quipped.

On the other hand, at the 2015 Monaco Grand Prix, Verstappen suffered a high-speed collision with Romain Grosjean after glancing into the back of the Lotus car on the approach to Turn 1 at Sainte Devote (built in honor of Saint Devota, a fourth-century martyr and the patron saint of Monaco, although the monastery is typically covered with crash barriers and advertising signs during the race). Verstappen's vehicle flew nose-first into the buffers at high speed, but he escaped unscathed.

Verstappen was given a five-place grid penalty for supposedly causing the accident (though he blamed Grosjean for braking earlier than he had on the previous lap, thus catching him "off guard") and was subsequently labeled "dangerous" by Williams driver Felipe Massa. Verstappen didn't hesitate to hit back at Massa by pointing out that the Brazilian pilot had also been involved in a similar incident with Sergio Perez at the 2014 Canadian Grand Prix.

However, a second season with Red Bull's junior squad began in fine style for Max with three finishes for points in his first three races. Yet the desire to challenge for bigger prizes was clearly evident. Just before the Spanish Grand Prix, the youngster was drafted into the Red Bull racing line-up for the major race.

On May 5, 2016, following the Russian Grand Prix, Red Bull announced that Verstappen would be replacing Daniil Kvyat from the Spanish Grand Prix, with Kvyat going back to Toro Rosso. According to the Red Bull team's principal, Christian Horner, "Max has proven to be an outstanding young talent. His performance at Toro Rosso has been impressive so far and we are pleased to give him the opportunity to drive for Red Bull Racing."

His immediate contribution was nothing short of sensational. He qualified in third and then drove a flawless race in Spain to claim his first F1 victory, becoming the sport's youngest-ever competition winner, despite later confessing that he wasn't completely sure what all the fancy buttons on the steering wheel were supposed to do.

In that race on Spanish soil, Verstappen cruised into second place behind teammate, Daniel Ricciardo, on the opening lap after Mercedes teammates, Lewis Hamilton and Nico Rosberg, had conveniently crashed out of the race. Verstappen finally took the lead after being put on a two-stop refueling strategy, rather than a three-stop one like Ricciardo.

Max held off Ferrari's hard-charging Kimi Raikkonen in the final stages of the race to secure his first Formula One victory. By doing so, he replaced Sebastian Vettel as the youngest driver ever to win an F1 Grand Prix at precisely 18 years and 228 days.

The Dutchman was then able to take his win tally into double figures and soon established himself as a true championship contender. The following year, he finished third in the Drivers' Championship, scoring wins in the 70th Anniversary Grand Prix at Silverstone, England, as well as the season finale in the Abu Dhabi desert. He displayed astounding consistency in 2020, ending up on the podium 11 times in the 12 races where he saw the checkered flag.

Red Bull's motorsport advisor, Helmut Marko, from Austria was particularly vocal in his praise of Verstappen, calling the youngster "light years ahead" of many of his Formula One rivals. Comparisons were even made to such bright stars as the late F1 icon, Brazilian speedster, Ayrton Senna, who passed away after a 1994 crash in Imola, Italy. Speaking of these parallels, did Verstappen feel the pressure?

"No, not really," Max admitted. "I don't look too far ahead. I think at the moment it's too early to talk about that stuff. I mean, as a driver, you know what to do. You just think hard and focus on what you have to do—drive the car fast around the track. You just have to focus on yourself and try to do the best possible job.

And keep your feet on the ground, that's important," he concluded.

It may be hard to keep your feet on the ground when the car you're in is almost flying. No doubt, Senna was a national hero in the massive F1-mad country of Brazil. Verstappen looks to achieve something similar in the slightly smaller European nation known as the Netherlands. In fact, he was crowned the 2016 Sportsman of the Year in Holland. "I'm very happy to represent my country," Max effused. "They're very passionate fans."

Indeed, it was Helmut Marko himself, the head of Red Bull Racing's driver development program and proven talent scout, who rescued Max from relative obscurity, just as he had done with Sebastian Vettel, Daniel Ricciardo, and Daniil Kyvat before him.

The announcement of Max's promotion was met with a certain degree of surprise and intrigue and a good measure of stinging criticism from Jacques Villeneuve as well. The French-Canadian, who became world champion in 1997, was never one to offer a sweet-smelling bouquet when a baseball bat would do instead.

"I think Max is an insult. Does Red Bull realize it's putting a child in Formula 1? Before you start playing with the lives of others, you have to learn, and it's just not Formula 1's role to teach," Villeneuve ranted to the Italian motorsport magazine, *Omnicorse*.

Max was quick to defend himself: "In the end, age is just a number." Tall (well, relatively so as F1 drivers go, at 5'9" or 1.81 m.) and lean, with well-defined cheekbones clearly passed down from his Dutch father, the younger Verstappen praised his sponsor: "The Red Bull Driver program prepares you well. I feel like I'm ready and I feel like I belong in Formula One. I've been chosen because Toro Rosso and Red Bull believe in me. And I aim to repay them by not letting them down.

"If I didn't think I was good enough, if Red Bull didn't think I was good enough, I wouldn't be in Formula One. Some people have said that to step into Formula One after just one season of car racing is too soon, but I want to prove those people wrong," the alleged 'child' concluded.

To counter the caustic criticism of Jacques Villeneuve, just consider the musings of British TV broadcaster, Martin Brundle, who's announced F1 races for practically two decades. "We've got a megastar on our hands in the making here. What confidence in the car," he enthused about Max. "Verstappen will be in a world championship-winning team before he's 20. He's showing all the hallmarks of a Senna, of a Schumacher, in my view."

IS RED BULL MORE THAN AN ENERGY DRINK?

The idea of building and playing (in this case driving) with a team in F1 racing isn't quite as clear as in basketball or football. Max's 'team' started with his parents when he was young, in particular his dad—despite what some have dubbed as the elder's unorthodox approach.

"I've always had my Dad with me. He was my mechanic, my coach, and my engine tuner, so we've done everything together. I think that was a great help for me. Sometimes fathers are always positive about their sons, but you also have to be straight and honest. That is what we have between us. He pushes me in only the things that he and I both know I can do better," Max clarified.

Naturally, Jos wasn't hesitant to weigh in on the debate about age as a proud father and someone who recognizes, like nobody else, his son's outstanding skills at the controls of an ultra-modern F1 car. Strapped into a multi-faceted, energy-boosting, hybrid power unit, with bucket loads of downforce and almost 900 'brake horsepower' (bhp) under his slender right foot, capable of achieving velocities upwards of 205 mph (or 330 kph), it's a great deal for a 17-year-old, or anyone for that matter, to handle.

Just for your info, a typical family car in the U.S. produces about 180 to 200 horsepower under the hood. Brake horsepower differs slightly from simple horsepower in that the former also takes power loss due to friction inside an engine into account.

"People who criticize Max for being in Formula One because of his age-— those people don't know Max. Of course, they're waiting to see how he handles the pressure of Formula One, and maybe waiting for him to fail. I've been working with him on his racing for the past 10 years. He has so much more experience than other seventeen-year-old kids. He's been around motorsport since he was a child. It is his life. We have done everything ourselves up until the moment we signed with Red Bull," father Verstappen claimed.

Regardless of his age, Max had by then become a member of the elite Red Bull F1 racing team and thus had to act accordingly. But just how do F1 teams function when they apparently have two different cars competing against each other in the same race?

On the track, there are always tactics and strategies that take both drivers into consideration. For example, if it benefits one driver (and the team) more to get to the podium than the other in any given race, then the latter will be instructed to let the former pass, and refueling pit stops will be timed in accordance.

Off the track, the two drivers are fundamentally divided into two separate teams. They have their own mechanics for their respective cars, along with personal physiotherapists and coaches and engineers who focus on only one car, not both. It's also worth noting that the two drivers are chosen primarily for their driving skills. Their personalities and, as a result, potential personality conflicts aren't considered too pertinent.

The drivers themselves need to hone in on their own performance, which means maintaining top fitness, both mental and physical, and paying attention to instructions from their team while out on the track. Obviously, these aren't tasks that can be easily shared.

And what about F1 championships, points, trophies, and money, you ask? When teammates finish a race first and second, the driver who cops the checkered flag receives 25 points, while the other scores 18 points. The team itself accumulates 43 points. Drivers get paid no matter how good their output is. On the other hand, teams only receive payouts from the race's and sport's profits when they score more points than other teams.

Of course, Max has been an integral part of numerous teams since his early karting days. Earlier on in 2021, Verstappen was asked to single out his favorite teammate, especially if he were to choose between Australian Daniel Riccardo (who'd decided to move on from Red Bull and sign with Renault, and later with McClaren) and the more recent Sergio Perez (who'd been recruited to replace Riccardo). Max appeared diplomatic in recognizing various running mates over the years.

"I don't know," Verstappen admitted to Sky Sport. "I think Daniel—he was outstanding. Of course, back then, I was a bit younger and a bit more inexperienced, so it's difficult to compare the two. I find it very difficult to always talk about that because I had a great relationship with Pierre (Gasly), and I had a great relationship with Alex (Albon). They were great drivers as well. I have a good relationship with Checo and it's going really well. We are leading the Constructors' (Championship) and I hope we can keep that up."

At first glance, it seemed Gasly could never quite rise to meet the expectations of Red Bull and was sent back to Toro Rosso (now Alpha Tauri) after only 12 starts with the Bull. At the same time, we fans aren't usually privy to the politics behind the scenes. Still, the Frenchmen exacted his revenge in the following years, mounting three podiums, including a win with Alpha Tauri to solidify his standing.

"He feels really good in the Alpha Tauri car and it's great to see him qualify in fifth, sixth, and getting good results," Verstappen gushed. "Even the win last year—I'm very happy for him."

MAX'S MAJOR CRASH

In 2018, having already bashed wheels two times during an increasingly taut race-long showdown, the Red Bull drivers' days were cut short after a heavy collision on Lap 40 of the Azerbaijan Grand Prix. Riccardo smacked into the back of Verstappen as he attempted to pass entering Turn One. Wait...weren't they two Red Bull teammates at the time? Weren't they supposed to be working together to benefit and win for the team?

The nation known as Azerbaijan, a former Soviet republic, is bounded by the Caspian Sea and the Caucasus Mountains, spanning Asia and Europe. Its capital, Baku, is famed for its walled 'Inner City' dating from medieval ages.

After the race, the Baku stewards summoned the drivers to go through the incident, and later issued reprimands to both Ricciardo and Verstappen, though the pair escaped presumably damaging grid demotions for the following race in Spain.

The judges decided that while Verstappen had made "two moves" in front of Ricciardo and the "incident had its origins in the moves", they determined that both were "relatively minor" on the Dutchman's part. On top of that, Ricciardo admitted "he left his move to overtake on the left too late", and hence the judging panel ruled that his actions "also contributed to the incident".

Both drivers voiced regret for the collision, according to race stewards. Verstappen and Ricciardo had already made individual apologies to the Red Bull group in TV interviews. Still unimpressed, Christian Horner stressed that the drivers shared equal responsibility for the crash and confirmed that the pair would need to formally apologize to the whole team at their Milton Keynes factory before the next race in Barcelona.

"We allow them to race, we allow them to go wheel to wheel. We discussed in the pre-race meetings about giving each other space, and this was the culmination of two guys taking things into their own hands, which shouldn't have happened," Horner quipped. "They're both in the doghouse; you can see that in their body language, and they will be in the factory to apologize to all the staff prior to the Barcelona race."

The reprimands were the drivers' firsts during that particular season. An F1 driver is handed a 10-place grid penalty if they rack up three such warnings in a single campaign, provided that at least two were for driving offenses. At the moment the crash occurred, Verstappen and Ricciardo were sitting in fourth and fifth places respectively in what proved to be an unexpectedly tough race for Red Bull.

The double retirement, which was the team's second in the space of four races in that campaign, meant they missed out on at least 22 points. At that juncture, Red Bull trailed leader, Ferrari, by 59 points in the Constructors' Championship, while the team's lead point scorer, Ricciardo, dropped 33 points behind Lewis Hamilton, the race's ultimate winner, in the Drivers' Championship.

Red Bull's head honcho, Horner, tried to keep the sense of team above all when he took both drivers to task: "I'm not apportioning blame one way or the other to either of the drivers—they're both to blame in this, and it's the team that unfortunately misses out."

Maybe in an effort to inspire his team for the following race, Horner brought back the memory of Michael Schumacher in his unstoppable prime. The German ace was able to rally the Ferrari team together in the 1990s—a team that hadn't previously won a championship since 1979.

That team was suffering in all areas and aspects, from the board room to the pit lane. Schumacher's superlative story is one of strong leadership, intricate teamwork, and subtle strategy. He managed to pull a team out of the doldrums and became known as one of the best drivers in F1 history in the painstaking process.

In the short-term analysis, Verstappen was involved in "incidents" at four races in 2018 and scored just 18 points, leaving him eighth in the standings. At the very least, he had a lot of lucky number eights and eighteens to his credit that year.

THE SKY IS VERSTAPPEN'S LIMIT

Leading up to the 2021 race in Max's adopted hometown of Monaco, Covid-19 pandemic protocols had turned the usual playground of the rich and famous on the French Riviera into a relatively serene place, operating at a fraction of the overindulgence linked to motorsport's loudest and proudest display of conspicuous consumption. Yet, the tournament's competitive levels were still peaking.

Long seen as a knock against F1 and car racing in general, the fact that so much precious fuel is wasted, and so much ear-splitting noise is created in an extremely dangerous exhibition of sporting prowess, has yet to be reconciled. But for the time being, Max was apparently enjoying the weekend.

The moment was indeed a milestone: the 23-year-old Red Bull driver was engulfed in the first real World Championship slugfest of his six-year career. Yet to spy him calm and standing at the dock of the picturesque Port de Fontvieille harbor, you'd never have known it. There was an easy peace surrounding the Dutchman.

Such tranquility was by no means a characteristic you'd expect from a racer who possessed a no-holds-barred approach and paid little attention to his rivals' lofty reputations. From the start of his F1 career, Verstappen had been nothing but a winner—his first at the record-setting age of 18—and was frequently pegged as a future champion. However, it was only in 2021 that this burden of destiny had veered into the actual realm of possibility.

In 2020, new rules had suddenly leveled the playing field. Tire maker, Pirelli, had pinpointed worrisome aerodynamic overloads on the tires of F1's fastest-ever cars, and bodywork adjustments were mandated to dramatically reduce the downforce that 2021 cars were able to generate.

Those most seriously impacted were Mercedes, seven-time Constructors' Champions, and none other than Lewis Hamilton, their seven-time Drivers' Champion. The former mysterious alterations to floor dimensions and rear brake ducts were gone, immediately wiping out major pieces of the Silver Arrows' traditional advantage and brought the sport's dominant force suddenly within striking distance.

At the season opener in Bahrain, Verstappen quickly showed his burning intent by blazing into pole position, only to be strategically assaulted in the race by the cagey Hamilton, who lured the younger driver into a ruinous late overtake that ensured the win for the Brit.

Verstappen battled his way back in the next round in Imola, shoulder-muscling Lewis pole-sitter from the opening gun. The former blasted to an unchallenged victory, with his chief rival recovering to score second. This bruising encounter appeared to indicate that the Red Bull driver wouldn't be easily cowed, yet the next two rounds—in Portugal and Spain—witnessed winning masterclasses from the veteran Hamilton.

By contrast, Max's races were marred by minor mistakes: a momentary slide at Turn 14 in Portugal, an unclear call to the pits, and a front right wheel that locked up during his outgoing lap in Barcelona. In the closest competition F1 had seen in ten years, these were tiny misdeeds that were enough to give the glory again to the fearless superhero who sat in the Mercedes hot seat.

"You have to understand that if it's not your day, it's not your day, and you have to settle for a certain result," Max insisted. "Last year, or in the years before, we knew that we weren't in a championship fight, so in that situation, you go for every single opportunity to win it, or bin it. Well, not really, but you do go over the limit to try to get a better result.

"But we now have a car that's more capable of bringing the fight to Mercedes. It's more than just a one-weekend wonder. We have to make sure that even if we don't have a perfect weekend, we still score a lot of points. It's a different approach," the Red Bull challenger concluded.

Verstappen seemed a world away from the character who notoriously threatened to punch competitor Esteban Ocon after the Frenchman whacked into him during the 2018 Brazilian Grand Prix. This was somehow the same person who risked it all in a bruising, wheel-banging final thrust past Ferrari's Charles Leclerc to literally grab victory at the 2019 Austrian Grand Prix. The 2021 Verstappen version possessed one all-encompassing vision: it all came down to the closeness of the battle with Hamilton.

"I'm up against a seven-time world champion who has a lot of experience, but nevertheless, you try to beat him. When it's not possible, you settle for the best possible result because it is going to be a long season and we cannot afford to make any big mistakes," Max affirmed. "I know that Lewis is also very good at knowing how to pick his moments, at knowing when it's not happening but still getting the best possible result out of it."

The situation quickly became more difficult when Hamilton turned up the psychological warfare. When questioned further about the closeness of the on-track scuffles between the two, the Mercedes man tried to stick to the high ground. "I think I've done well to avoid all the incidents," he commented. "But we have 19 more (races) and we could connect. Max feels he perhaps has a lot to prove. I'm not in the same boat."

Max grinned from ear to ear, refusing to swallow the bait. "We've raced hard and avoided contact on both sides. Let's hope we can keep doing that, keep being on

track, and race hard against each other."
All's fair in love and F1.

F1 races in the modern age are complicated maneuvers in controlled technicality, involving fiendishly complex concepts of tire and vehicle management, fuel conservation, and tactical energy mobilization in hybrid powertrains. In other words, these are not just hybrid passenger cars you put on cruise control to kick back on the highway.

The race itself attracts the TV cameras and hauls in the fans. But the attempt to first qualify is much more basic: It's only the racer and the machine, with the minimum fuel load possible and complete commitment to the limits of adhesion. Especially in Max's Monaco hometown, at a tight winding track where passing others is practically impossible, the result is almost always defined by your grid position, and qualifying is basically everything.

Despite his blazing qualifying times during the weekend, Max qualified in second. Leclerc happened to clip the barriers at the principality's outdoor swimming pool. His Ferrari bashed hard into the barriers on the outside corner and the session was immediately red-flagged. Verstappen's lap was thus spoiled, and he'd be forced to line up second on the starting grid. But if he was flustered, he never once let on.

Chatting with the press afterward, Verstappen let the Ferrari driver off the hook, reiterating that he shouldn't have his pole position revoked. "It's different if someone does it deliberately, but that wasn't the case here," he quipped to reporters, those hovering with recording devices always ready, ever hungry for more controversy.

"We all push, and a mistake is easily made. All in all, everything is very positive. It's always better to start first, but I don't think we were only the second-fastest today. It's racing, and there is a possibility that there will be a red flag. Charles isn't doing it on purpose," Verstappen stressed. Max's mojo appeared intact.

MAKING TIME TO GIVE BACK

At about the same age as most young adults are getting out of college and fighting to find a suitable job, Max Verstappen is a world-famous race car driver with an estimated net worth of $60 million due to his numerous endorsement deals. He's committed to a Red Bull contract until 2023.

He also has legions of fans who call themselves the Orange Army. They're not too difficult to spot, displaying brilliant orange t-shirts at all European races. This kind of popularity clearly makes Max desirable among big brands, thus turning him into one of the most marketable drivers on the grid. His major sponsors include Jumbo Supermarkets, Ziggo, G-Star Raw, CarNext.com, as well as Red Bull.

In a video made for one of his sponsors, G-Star RAW, on his YouTube channel, Max talked about his eating habits. He'd already indicated that he often prefers to skip breakfast and practices intermittent fasting. But which dish really makes Verstappen happy?

He admitted to being a lover of Dutch and Italian cuisine, and also stressed that if he doesn't eat, he won't be able to find happiness. "But if I haven't eaten properly, I'll be grumpy," he warned.

Just in case you ever have Max over for dinner, Verstappen prefers to eat what he knows, and doesn't like to try new dishes: "But if I do that once, and I don't like it, I'll just order something else."

The driver also grooves on a variety of typical Dutch dishes: "I do like mashed potatoes. And I don't know if it's really Dutch, but when I'm with my mom or dad, I also like to have a French fries special, or a 'frikandel special' (a sort of minced-meat hot dog). I can enjoy that so much."

Similar to many F1 racers, Verstappen has participated in charity soccer events. He's also part of the Charity Stars and raced in a 2017 Red Bull-sponsored charity event. In early 2020, Verstappen donated an unknown amount to a fundraiser as an aid for koalas affected by Australian bushfires. Give him time—after all, Amazon's Jeff Bezos only got around to donating a few of his billions after age 60.

In the meantime, Brazilian model and journalist, Kelly Piquet, has more than a single connection to the sport of F1—as the daughter of a racing legend and after giving birth to a child with another driver—before dating Max. The 32-year-old began managing Formula E's social media back in 2015 and has been a race regular her entire adult life.

That all started, thanks to her famous and rapid father. Nelson Piquet won three World Drivers' Championships between 1981 and 1987, racing the first two with Brabham using a Ford engine before switching over to Williams with a Honda under the hood in his final triumph.

Better known for his playboy lifestyle away from the track, Nelson has now fathered seven children, with Kelly coming from his second marriage to Dutchwoman Sylvia Tamsma. The elder Piquet is currently with Vivianne de Souza Leao as we go to press.

Due to her strong connection to motorsport, Kelly met Russian race driver, Daniil Kvyat, with whom she shares a daughter named Penelope, who was born in 2019. The year after, a breakup occurred, and she began dating the Dutch youngster Verstappen, nine years her junior at age 23.

Kvyat competed in F1 from 2014 to 2017, and again from 2019 to 2020, racing under the Russian flag. He became the second-ever F1 driver from Russia, and ranks as the most successful of the four Russian drivers to date, with a total of three podiums.

Despite this current close connection to F1 icon, Nelson, Max said in June that he wouldn't necessarily be asking for any advice, as he looked to extend his 32-point lead over Lewis Hamilton that season.

"Of course, he's a legend in Formula 1. It is my own career," Max said simply. Perhaps, he'd turn first to his dad, or maybe his mom. But at the end of the day, the foot on the accelerator will decidedly be his own.

MORE FROM JACKSON CARTER BIOGRAPHIES

My goal is to spark the love of reading in young adults around the world. Too often children grow up thinking they hate reading because they are forced to read material they don't care about. To counter this we offer accessible, easy to read biographies about sportspeople that will give young adults the chance to fall in love with reading.

Go to the Website Below to Join Our Community

https://mailchi.mp/7cced1339ff6/jcbcommunity

Or Find Us on Facebook at

www.facebook.com/JacksonCarterBiographies

As a Member of Our Community You Will Receive:

First Notice of Newly Published Titles

Exclusive Discounts and Offers

Influence on the Next Book Topics

Don't miss out, join today and help spread the love of reading around the world!

OTHER WORKS BY JACKSON CARTER BIOGRAPHIES

Made in the USA
Las Vegas, NV
18 February 2022

44190448R00046